GEESE

Sandie Lee Books

Geese

Geese are waterfowl. They belong to the family of, Anatidae. These birds also have lots of other names. The female of this species is called, a goose, the male is, a gander and a group on the ground are called, a gaggle. When the birds are all flying together they can be a skein, wedge or team. But whatever name they go by, geese are amazing birds. Let's explore further to see what interesting facts we can discover.

Where in the World?

Did you know there are 29 different species of geese? These birds are found in North America, Asia and Europe. They like to live where there is water. This gives them more choices of food to eat and also helps keep them safe from predators. Geese will take to the water when they feel threatened.

The Body of a Goose

Did you know a goose has a long neck? The goose has short legs with two webbed feet. The head is slender with a powerful bill. Its eyes are small and set on the sides of its head. Geese can weigh around 25 pounds. It has feathers and strong wings.

What a Goose Eats

Did you know the goose is an omnivore? This means it eats plants and meat. The goose will eat small fish, insects, grubs, plankton and other small water life. The goose pulls the plants from the ground with its powerful bill. Some species can eat up to 4 pounds of grass in one day.

The Goose's Special Ability

Did you know most geese migrate? This means they will fly long distances to avoid the snow and cold of winter to find a warmer climate. Snow geese are able to fly a round trip of about 5,000 miles. These birds can also travel at speeds of 50 miles-per-hour.

The Goose as Prey

Did you know some wild animals hunt the goose's eggs? Predators like the fox and wild dogs will hunt adult geese. Raccoons and other small predators like to dine on the goose's eggs. Man also is a threat to the goose. This bird is used for its meat and for its feathers.

Goose Talk

Did you know a goose can make noises? A goose can make a loud honking sound and even hiss when it feels threatened. If these sounds don't work to scare off the predator, the goose will extend its wings, flap them really hard and run towards the person or animal.

Geese Molting

Did you know the goose's flight and tail feathers fall out to make room for new feathers? This is called molting. An adult goose will go through a molt in the months of June and July. During this time the goose will be unable to fly, so it must be near a body of water so it can make a quick escape.

Goose Mom

Did you know the goose makes a nest on the ground? The mother goose will build a nest in a safe location. She will then lay one egg each day until she is finished. Most goose moms have about 5 eggs, but some species can have up to 9. In about 30 days the baby geese will hatch from their eggs.

Baby Geese

Did you know a baby goose is called a gosling? Baby geese are born covered in fuzzy feathers. Some species are yellow in color. Within 24 hours of all the goslings hatching, the parents will lead the babies to water. They can't fly for a few months, but they are born knowing how to swim!

The Goose at Rest

Did you know some geese can sleep with 1 eye open? Since geese sleep on the ground, they must keep an eye open at all times. Geese also sleep in large groups to stay safe. You can tell when the geese are very relaxed as they will have their heads tucked under one of their wings.

Life of a Goose

Did you know that geese can have a long lifespan in the wild? Healthy geese can live to be upwards of 20 years-old. The male and female goose will pair up when they are 4 years-old and spend the rest of their lives together. This is called being, monogamous.

The Canada Goose

This species of goose has a long black neck and black head with white patches on its face. The rest of the body is a steel grey with white. The Canada goose can weigh around 20 pounds and is perhaps the most recognizable of all the goose species. They can eat up to 12 hours each day

The Nene

This goose is native to the Hawaiian Islands and is their state bird. It has a light grey body and neck with bands of black on it. Its head is mostly black with a black-colored bill. This bird can weigh around 15 pounds. It eats vegetation, leaves, seeds, flowers, fruits and shrubs. It can be seen most anywhere on the islands.

The Chinese Goose

This type of goose is domesticated. This means it was born and raised with humans. This bird weighs around 25 to 30 pounds and can be white or shades of brown. The male has a large knob-like growth on its upper bill. In the white Chinese goose, this will be a bright orange color.

Quiz

Question 1: What fun word is a group of geese called?

Answer 1: A gaggle

Question 2: Since the goose is an *omnivore,* what does it eat?

Answer 2: It will eat both plant matter and meat

Question 3: Snow geese fly around 5,000 miles each year. What are they doing?

Answer 3: *Migrating* to another place

Question 4: How do some geese sleep to stay safe?

Answer 4: With one eye open

Question 5: Which goose is the state bird of Hawaii?

Answer 5: The Nene goose

Thank you for checking out another addition from Sandie Lee Books! Make sure to check out Amazon.com for many other great titles.

www.ingramcontent.com/pod-product-compliance
Lightning Source LLC
Chambersburg PA
CBHW050801290526
45792CB00008B/2277